How to "Immunize" Children against Drug and Alcohol Abuse:

A Research-Based Guide
Focusing on Early Childhood

by Dr. Nouzar Nakhaee

To my mother
All I have is hers…

Title: How to "Immunize" Children against Drug and Alcohol Abuse
Subtitle: A Research-Based Guide Focusing on Early Childhood
Author: Dr. Nouzar Nakhaee
Illustrator: Saleh Razm-Hosseini
Publisher: American Academic Research, USA
ISBN: 9781947464148

2020 © Dr. Nouzar Nakhaee
All Rights Reserved for the Author

All rights reserved. No part of this book may be reprinted or reproduced utilized in any form or by any electronic, mechanical, or other means now known or hereafter invented, including photocopying and recording, or in any information storage or retrieval system, without permission in writing from the author.

Contents

- INTRODUCTION 5
- WHAT IS THE CRITICAL AGE FOR PREVENTATIVE MEASURES? 7
- WHAT FACTORS INCREASE OR DECREASE THE LIKELIHOOD FOR DRUG AND ALCOHOL ABUSE? 8
- RISK FACTORS RELATED TO PREGNANCY 9
- RISK FACTORS FOR INFANTS AND TODDLERS 9
- PROTECTIVE FACTORS 10
- FAMILY ENVIRONMENT 11
- THE ROLE OF HEREDITY 13
- AT WHAT AGES AND STAGES OF DEVELOPMENT IS THE RISK OF DRUG AND ALCOHOL ABUSE HIGHER? 14
- ARE GIRLS OR BOYS MORE VULNERABLE TO DRUG AND ALCOHOL ABUSE? 15
- NEGATIVE CHILDHOOD EXPERIENCES AND EARLY CHILDHOOD STRESS 16
- MAKING TIME FOR CHILD AND PARENTAL INVOLVEMENT 18
- EARLY MATERNAL SEPARATION (MS) 19
- ATTACHMENT STYLE DURING INFANCY 20
- PARENTING STYLE 21
- AUTHORITARIAN PARENTING (MORE CONTROL AND LESS AFFECTION) 21
- INDULGENT PARENTING (LESS CONTROL AND MORE AFFECTION) 22
- AUTHORITATIVE PARENTING (MORE CONTROL AND MORE AFFECTION) 22
- NEGLECTFUL PARENTING (LESS CONTROL AND LESS AFFECTION) 22
- POSITIVE PARENTING 23
- SELF-ESTEEM 26
- SELF-CONTROL 27
- STRENGTHENING EXECUTIVE FUNCTIONS 29
- REINFORCE THE ASSERTIVENESS AND SKILL OF SAYING "NO" 33
- PEER INFLUENCE 34
- DO NOT OVERLOOK THE IMPACT OF FILMS 35
- NURTURE THE CHILD'S SPIRITUALITY 36

Acknowledgements

I am especially grateful to Lynn Terry Ph.D. for editing consultation. This book would not have taken shape without her help. I can never thank Mans Forouzi for all she has done for me. The caricatures in this book are the work of my friend and award-winning artist Muhammad Saleh Razm- Hosseini.

I would like to thank my wife Rauzyeh, and my two sons Muhammad and Amin, who sacrificed a lot of their free times and holidays to provide me the quality time needed to write this book.

Nouzar Nakhaee, M.D., M.P.H.
Professor of Community Medicine
Kerman Neuroscience Research Center

"It is easier to build strong children than to repair broken men." – Fredrick Douglass

Introduction

The family is the foundation for prevention of drug and alcohol abuse. The FDA defines drug abuse as: "the intentional, non-therapeutic use of a drug product or substance, even once, to achieve a desired psychological or physiological effect".[1] Family and especially childhood environmental circumstances must be the focus in order to prevent drug and alcohol abuse.[2]

Alcohol and drug use are socially acquired behaviors and individuals begin to learn social behaviors from early childhood in the family setting. Children's appropriate and inappropriate behaviors gradually develop from early childhood through observation of and communication with parents and other people. According to social learning theory and primary socialization theory, the family is the first and most important pillar of learning of the set of norms, values and behaviors. In general, children's behaviors are influenced by two main factors. Both of these factors are inherited from or influenced by parents, i.e. nature and nurture; also referred to as genes and environment.

---

[1] Food and Drug Administration Center for Drug Evaluation and Research (CDER). Assessment of Abuse Potential of Drugs Guidance for Industry. 2017.
[2] Jadidi N, Nakhaee N. Etiology of drug abuse: a narrative analysis. Journal of addiction. 2014.

Recommendations written in this book are, in fact, "behavioral vaccines"[1], i.e. if we observe a set of principles during the golden age of early childhood, children can be substantially immunized against drug and alcohol abuse as they age.[2] Telling teenagers about the dangers of drug and alcohol abuse as a preventative measure is not supported by scientific evidence.[3] This book attempts to, in everyday language, provide families with drug and alcohol abuse prevention strategies based on the latest scientific evidence. Given the emphasis of recent research on the importance and effectiveness of preventative interventions in early childhood, this book focuses on children ages zero to eight.[4]

According to social learning theory, the family is the first and most important pillar of learning of the set of norms, values and behaviors.

---

[1] Embry DD. Behavioral vaccines and evidence-based kernels: nonpharmaceutical approaches for the prevention of mental, emotional, and behavioral disorders. Psychiatric Clinics. 2011 Mar 1;34(1):1-34.
[2] Velleman RD, Templeton LJ, Copello AG. The role of the family in preventing and intervening with substance use and misuse: a comprehensive review of family interventions, with a focus on young people. Drug and alcohol review. 2005 Mar 1;24(2):93-109.
[3] Stockings E, Hall WD, Lynskey M, Morley KI, Reavley N, Strang J, Patton G, Degenhardt L. Prevention, early intervention, harm reduction, and treatment of substance use in young people. The Lancet Psychiatry. 2016 Mar 1;3(3):280-96.
[4] National Institute on Drug Abuse, National Institutes of Health. Principles of substance abuse prevention for early childhood, a research-based guide. 2016.

What is the Critical Age for Preventative Measures?

The influence of childhood development is the dominate force when considering health strategies. The focus on children from birth to eight years old is essential in order to have a vibrant and lively community with a minimum of mental health problems. Although preventing any health problem at any age is important and necessary, the most effective time for intervention begins with pre-pregnancy and continues from pregnancy and early childhood.

The brain connections are mainly formed during these periods and the effect of the underlying factor or factors protecting against drug and alcohol abuse is greater than with post-adolescents.

By adolescence the personality of the child is largely shaped.[1] Moreover, child behavior is predominately managed and monitored by parents. The young child, unlike adolescents and young people, has not discovered or experienced the world beyond the home or the alluring capacity of social media. In other words, although the first experience of drug abuse and alcohol consumption occurs after the age of ten, the underlying factors affecting drug and alcohol abuse appear in the first few years of life and even before birth.

---

[1] Allik J, Laidra K, Realo A, Pullmann H. Personality development from 12 to 18 years of age: Changes in mean levels and structure of traits. European Journal of Personality. 2004 Sep;18(6):445-62.

Conception to age eight is the most effective period for preventing drug and alcohol abuse.

What Factors Increase or Decrease the Likelihood for Drug and Alcohol Abuse?

Factors increasing the likelihood of drug and alcohol abuse are called risk factors, while the ones which decrease the probability of drug and alcohol abuse are considered protective factors. Some of these factors are inherent, such as genetic composition and personality, whereas others are related to the environment; parenting style and persistent and severe environmental stress. This stress can be the result of parent's mental illness. [1,2,3]

---

[1] Meque I, Salom C, Betts KS, Alati R. Predictors of Alcohol Use Disorders Among Young Adults: A Systematic Review of Longitudinal Studies. Alcohol and Alcoholism. 2019 Apr 3;54(3):310-24.

[2] Gray KM, Squeglia LM. Research Review: What have we learned about adolescent substance use? Journal of Child Psychology and Psychiatry. 2018 Jun;59(6):618-27.

[3] Nomura Y, Gilman SE, Buka SL. Maternal smoking during pregnancy and risk of alcohol use disorders among adult offspring. Journal of studies on alcohol and drugs. 2011 Mar;72(2):199-209.

Risk Factors Related To Pregnancy
- Hereditary transmission of drug and alcohol abuse through parental genes
- Drug, alcohol and/or tobacco use during pregnancy
- Maternal stress during pregnancy
- Violence against the pregnant mother

Maternal smoking during pregnancy increases the risk of drug and alcohol abuse disorder in the offspring.

Risk Factors for Infants and Toddlers
- Restless infants who cry inconsolably
- Insecure attachment style
- Nervous children who constantly fight
- Children with Attention-Deficit Hyperactivity Disorder (ADHD) and depression
- Severe and persistent stress at home such as poverty, parental mental illness and physical and emotional abuse of the child.

Nervous and violent children are at increased risk for drug and alcohol abuse in adult life.

Protective Factors

- A house full of affection
- Responsive child care – matching care-giving to the child's needs
- Parents' negative attitude toward drugs and alcohol

A fully affectionate family

Family Environment

The family must have an anti-drug and alcohol atmosphere, i.e. the child, from early childhood, understands that his parents have a negative attitude toward drug and alcohol abuse. Some parents mistakenly assume letting their children taste alcohol at home will protect them against abusive drinking.[1]

Scientific literature repeatedly states the reverse effects of this belief. Drug and alcohol abuse should not be ignored but rather condemned at opportunities such as while traveling, watching movies and interacting with drug and alcohol abusers.

Following this advice children and adolescents are less likely to consider drug and alcohol a normal behavior. An uneasy atmosphere at home, as well as severe marital disputes, also increases the likelihood of drug and alcohol abuse at an early age.[2]

The supervisory role of parents is vitally important in this regard. There are four Cs of parental supervision that forms a supportive family atmosphere.[3] **C**lear rules, **C**ontinuous communication, **C**onditions and **C**onsistency:

<u>Clear decisive and restrictive yet understandable rules:</u>
- Don't go to your friend's home alone.
- No friends are allowed at home if I am not home.

---

[1] Dickinson DM, Hayes KA, Jackson C, Ennett ST, Lawson C. Promoting an alcohol-free childhood: A novel home-based parenting program. American journal of health education. 2014 Mar 1;45(2):119-28.

[2] Yap MB, Cheong TW, Zaravinos-Tsakos F, Lubman DI, Jorm AF. Modifiable parenting factors associated with adolescent alcohol misuse: a systematic review and meta-analysis of longitudinal studies. Addiction. 2017 Jul;112(7):1142-62.

[3] Family Checkup: Positive Parenting Prevents Drug Use | National Institute on Drug Abuse (NIDA). 2012.

- **Continuous and intimate communication with the child.** You understand the dangers faced by your child better than the child and are aware of the child's opinions and intervene in a timely manner.
- **Make sure the child observes the rules and the Conditions surrounding the child are safe.** In many cases experience with alcohol and drugs is entirely innocent. Parents need to be watchful. For instance, when children attend a birthday party, parents need to verify the host parents are in agreement with their parenting policies.
- **Rules must be observed Consistently.** Flexibility and leniency are the antithesis of consistency and should be avoided.

The family must provide an anti-drug and alcohol atmosphere. The child, from early childhood, will understand that his parents' negative attitude toward drug and alcohol use is the standard for the family.

The Role of Heredity

Studies with twins show hereditary transmission can play a role in abuse of all drugs, from tobacco to opium and alcohol. Just as a child inherits many facial features, including hair and eye color, from his or her parents, drug use and alcohol consumption can be partially due to inheritance. Inheritability of addiction ranges from 40% to 60%.[1] The significance of the role heredity alerts parents to employ preventative measures when dealing with drug and alcohol abuse in the paternal or maternal family.

Hair and eye color are inherited from parents and there are hereditary factors related to inheritance of drug and alcohol abuse.

---

[1] Meyers JL, Dick DM. Genetic and environmental risk factors for adolescent-onset substance use disorders. Child and Adolescent Psychiatric Clinics. 2010 Jul 1;19(3):465-77.

At What Ages and Stages of Development is the Risk of Drug and Alcohol Abuse Higher?

Generally speaking, drug and alcohol abuse is more likely to occur at the age and stage when children age into late childhood and adolescence. Children undergo dramatic changes. These changes occur in terms of puberty and drastic environmental changes such as changing schools or parental divorce.

A study with 5000 people in 11 different countries indicate the risk of sensation seeking behaviors, such as drug and alcohol abuse, starts at the age of 10 and reaches its peak between the ages of 18 and 21.[1]

However, the risk of experimenting with drugs and alcohol may continue to the age of 50. It is generally stated that if one does not abuse drugs and alcohol by the age of 21 then the likelihood of drug and alcohol abuse decreases significantly.[2] Therefore the age range from 10 to 21 is vitally important.

---

[1] Steinberg L, Icenogle G, Shulman EP, Breiner K, Chein J, Bacchini D, Chang L, Chaudhary N, Giunta LD, Dodge KA, Fanti KA. Around the world, adolescence is a time of heightened sensation seeking and immature self-regulation. Developmental science. 2018 Mar;21(2):e12532.

[2] Solter A. Raising drug-free kids: 100 tips for parents. Da Capo Lifelong Books; 2006 Aug 29.

The most critical age for decisions about drug use occur for youth between the ages of 10 to 21 years

Are Girls or Boys more Vulnerable to Drug and Alcohol Abuse?

Unlike girls, boys are influenced more by peers.[1] Although boys are more likely to abuse drugs and alcohol than girls, research indicates that if girls experience drug and alcohol use –from cigarettes, hookah, methamphetamines and alcohol –they move more quickly than boys towards drug and alcohol addiction.[2]

---

[1] de Boer A, Peeters M, Koning I. An experimental study of risk taking behavior among adolescents: A closer look at peer and sex influences. The Journal of Early Adolescence. 2017 Oct;37(8):1125-41.
[2] United Nations Office on Drugs and Crime (UNODC). World Drug Report 2018.

Although boys are more likely to initiate drug and alcohol use, after initiation girls move faster than boys towards drug addiction!

Negative Childhood Experiences and Early Childhood Stress

Negative childhood experiences include traumatic events a child experiences before the age of 18.

The earlier the child experiences these traumatic events the more likely the adverse effects on different aspects of the child's health and future development.[1] Maternal stress during pregnancy can also result in toddler behavior problems. Prenatal and antenatal domestic violence doubles the likelihood of problematic behavior in a 42-month-old child.[2]

---

[1] Hughes K, Bellis MA, Sethi D, Andrew R, Yon Y, Wood S, Ford K, Baban A, Boderscova L, Kachaeva M, Makaruk K. Adverse childhood experiences, childhood relationships and associated substance use and mental health in young Europeans. European journal of public health. 2019 Mar 20

[2] Flach C, Leese M, Heron J, Evans J, Feder G, Sharp D, Howard LM. Antenatal domestic violence, maternal mental health and subsequent child behaviour: a cohort study. BJOG: An International Journal of Obstetrics & Gynaecology. 2011 Oct;118(11):1383-91.

Childhood toxic stresses have various forms. These include losing a mother or caregiver, living in a family with socioeconomic problems, exposure to repeated parental struggles. Most important toxic stress includes neglect of a young child and physical, emotional or sexual abuse. In fact, devastating effects of childhood stress are reflected in adolescence. Childhood adversities increase the risk of alcohol or marijuana use before the age of 10 by a factor of 4 and a factor of 12 times respectively.[1]

The lack of an emotionally sound life for a child can result in the likelihood of drug and alcohol abuse as the child ages.

---

[1] Andersen SL. Stress, sensitive periods, and substance abuse. Neurobiol Stress. 2019 (10).

Making Time for Child and Parental Involvement

From preschool to age 8 a child has more than 300 days out of school for holidays. How many of these days do parents spend with their children? There are many opportunities to interact in the following ways:

Playing together, eating meals together, telling stories, watching cartoons, going to the park or creating adventures in nature – to name a few.

Studies indicate the more time parents spend with children, especially in the early years, then less time is needed in adulthood.[1]

Children are less likely to abuse drugs and alcohol and associate with inappropriate peers when they grow up with loving parents who are an active part of their lives.[2]

The quality of time we spend with a child is more important than the quantity of time. Think quality not quantity!

---

[1] Hayakawa M, Giovanelli A, Englund MM, Reynolds AJ. Not just academics: Paths of longitudinal effects from parent involvement to substance abuse in emerging adulthood. Journal of Adolescent Health. 2016 Apr 1;58(4):433-9.

[2] Mynttinen M, Pietilä AM, Kangasniemi M. What Does Parental Involvement Mean in Preventing Adolescents' Use of Alcohol? An Integrative Review. Journal of Child & Adolescent Substance Abuse. 2017 Jul 4;26(4):338-51.

Early Maternal Separation (MS)

Following the Second World War when many children lost their mothers, the World Health Organization launched a program to investigate the effects of MS on children. However, this research did not proceed.

The second wave of research regarding MS occurred in the early 21st century due to modernization of society and the expansion of a culture of individualism.

There is overwhelming evidence of a relationship between MS and drug and alcohol abuse in adulthood. This effect association has been proven in most animal studies.

Studies with humans indicate similar results.[1] MS has lasting effects on the brain and these negative aspects would not be compensated by a later.[2]

Early Maternal Separation in infants is a predisposing factor for future drug and alcohol abuse.

---

[1] Delavari F, Sheibani V, Esmaeili-Mahani S, Nakhaee N. Maternal separation and the risk of drug abuse in later life. Addiction & health. 2016 Apr;8(2):107.

[2] Feng X, Wang L, Yang S, Qin D, Wang J, Li C, Lv L, Ma Y, Hu X. Maternal separation produces lasting changes in cortisol and behavior in rhesus monkeys. Proceedings of the National Academy of Sciences. 2011 Aug 23;108(34):14312-7.

Attachment Style during Infancy

Early bonding between the child and the mother or the child's primary caregiver has long-term effects on mental health and function during adulthood.[1]

Naturally, human babies are heavily dependent on their mothers and their brains are about one-third the size of the adult brain.

Childhood experiences with the primary caregiver have a significant impact on the child's natural brain wiring. The child's paramount need is affection; not expensive toys or a room full of stuff. It is critical for a child to experience a close relationship with a sensitive and caring primary caregiver. This relationship fosters a child's feeling of safety. A meta-analysis of 56721 people revealed a lack of secure attachment could be one of the predisposing factors leading to drug and alcohol abuse in adolescence.[2]

Infants tend to cling to their mother or primary caregivers and feel safe in their company. Meeting this emotional need is the basis for future positive mental health.

---

[1] Winston R, Chicot R. The importance of early bonding on the long-term mental health and resilience of children. London journal of primary care. 2016 Jan 2;8(1):12-4.

[2] Fairbairn CE, Briley DA, Kang D, Fraley RC, Hankin BL, Ariss T. A meta-analysis of longitudinal associations between substance use and interpersonal attachment security. Psychological bulletin. 2018 May;144(5):532.

Parenting Style

As discussed previously, parenting style plays an important part in the child's development.

There are four styles to discuss further:

authoritarian parenting (more control and less affection), indulgent parenting (less control and more affection), authoritative parenting (more control and more affection) and neglectful parenting (less control and less affection).

Authoritarian Parenting (more control and less affection)

This style includes strict, bad tempered parents who beat their children. It should be noted that not all authoritarian parents beat their children, but they are not close to their children and show no affection. They do this because they think if they show love for their children then they will spoil them.

Studies reveal the warmth of parent-child relationship together with monitoring has a protective effect on drug and alcohol abuse in adolescence.[1]

---

[1] Rusby JC, Light JM, Crowley R, Westling E. Influence of parent–youth relationship, parental monitoring, and parent substance use on adolescent substance use onset. Journal of family psychology. 2018 Apr;32(3):310.

Indulgent Parenting (less control and more affection)

This style of parenting is the exact opposite of the authoritarian style.

Parents in this category are not serious or strict. Indulgent parents are very attentive to their children's needs. They have no rules at home and do not beat their children. Children of indulgent parents are not expected to take responsibilities at home. This style of parenting usually produces spoiled children. Indulgent parents are unwilling to put some restrictions on their children and really want to love their children as much as they can without limiting them.

Authoritative Parenting
(more control and more affection)

This style of parenting is characterized by a combination of affection and warmth on one hand and demand, expectation and supervision on the other hand. Not only do authoritative parents establish their authority at home and give their children some responsibilities, but also love and care about them. Parents may hold children responsible for their mischief, but they never punish them physically. Instead they talk with their children about their misbehavior and guide them to more appropriate behavior.

Neglectful Parenting (less control and less affection)

Neglectful parents spend little time with their children. They lack a deep understanding of their children. Factors such as a busy life, depression and alcohol or drug addiction cause this neglectful behavior.

Applying rigorous and dictatorial parenting styles and showing little love and affection, authoritarian parents raise children with low dignity and self-esteem. On the other hand, indulgent parents believe buying excessive amounts of toys for their children means love, and, unfortunately these parents expect nothing from their children. These parents may even do the children's tasks for them.

The most successful parenting style. i.e. the authoritative style features parent's actions based on love, and at the same time, hold children responsible for their behavior. Parents strengthen their relationship with their children through affection and intimacy instead of instruction and force; simultaneously, they give their children responsibilities proportional to their age.

What your child needs is your presence, not your presents!

Positive parenting

Positive parenting has moved away from a risk factor model towards a more focus on predictors of positive outcomes.

"Positive parenting is the continual relationship of a parent(s) and a child or children that includes caring, teaching, leading, communicating, and providing for the needs of a child consistently and unconditionally".[1]

Children who spend their childhood in a positive parenting environment are believed less likely to abuse alcohol and drugs.[2]

Give children the opportunity and power to choose. Instead of dictating commands, give them a choice. For example, instead of forcing the child to drink milk, ask the child, "Which cup do you want to use for your milk?" Let children explore their surrounding world from the time they can crawl. Parents must keep children's environment very safe and not tell them where to go and where not to go. When children learn to make decisions on small tasks, they gradually learn responsibility for their own decisions.

Don't break a child's heart in childhood, otherwise the child will break the parent's heart in adulthood.

---

[1] Seay A, Freysteinson WM, McFarlane J. Positive parenting. InNursing Forum 2014 Jul (Vol. 49, No. 3, pp. 200-208).

[2] Luk JW, King KM, McCarty CA, McCauley E, Stoep AV. Prospective effects of parenting on substance use and problems across Asian/Pacific Islander and European American youth: tests of moderated mediation. Journal of studies on alcohol and drugs. 2017 Jul 26;78(4):521-30.

Children should feel that their good behavior is monitored and noted at home, i.e. when they clean up their toys without being prompted. The following are the basis of positive parenting:[1]

<u>Unconditional Love:</u> Assure children they are loved in all circumstances. Children do not need to show good behavior to be loved!

<u>Availability:</u> Parents do not need to spend all their time with their children. It means to be available when children need help or attention.

<u>Realistic Expectations:</u> Parents should expect children to do as much as they can. These parental expectations are based on age appropriate development; such as learning to walk and toilet training. Parents must avoid humiliating and frustrating words: dumb, stupid, crazy, lazy or bad.

<u>On being a parent:</u> Parents can treat children patiently if the home environment is calm and there is an abundance of adequate nutrition, sleep and recreation.

---

[1] Sanders MR. Development, evaluation, and multinational dissemination of the Triple P-Positive Parenting Program. Annu Rev Clin Psychol. 2012;8:345–379.

26 How to "Immunize" Children against Drug and Alcohol Abuse

Unconditional Love: Assure children they are loved in all circumstances. Children do not need to be well behaved to be loved!

Self-esteem

Adolescents with high self-esteem are less likely to abuse drugs and alcohol.[1]

Low self-esteem is a characteristic of children who are frustrated by the slightest failure, as well as those who are afraid to express their beliefs and opinions. To raise a child's self-esteem, show the child the they are loved and are important.

Take their opinions into consideration while making family decisions and then thank the child when a goal is accomplished. A child will not benefit from excessive support. A parent should avoid solving problems for children.

---

[1] Richardson CG, Kwon JY, Ratner PA. Self-esteem and the initiation of substance use among adolescents. Canadian journal of public health. 2013 Jan 1;104(1):e60-3.

Let them experience failure.[1] If children are shown their positive characteristics and weak points, in order to correct them, children gradually view themselves positively. Giving children agency plays a key role in formation of self-esteem and in the prevention of addiction.

My feeling of myself is called self-esteem. Adolescents with high self-esteem are less likely to abuse drugs and alcohol.

Self-control

Self-control is the child's ability to delay desire for better future conditions, or the ability to control thoughts, feelings and behaviors. A person with self-control can forgo the small immediate pleasure and wait for a greater reward. The child's ability to resist desire, control impulsive behaviors and delay satisfaction is enhanced by building self-control skills.[2] Consider the following principles to reinforce children's self-control:

---

[1] Brummelman E, Nelemans SA, Thomaes S, Orobio de Castro B. When parents' praise inflates, children's self-esteem deflates. Child development. 2017 Nov;88(6):1799-809.

[2] Daly M, Egan M, Quigley J, Delaney L, Baumeister RF. Childhood self-control predicts smoking throughout life: evidence from 21,000 cohort study participants. Health Psychology. 2016 Nov;35(11):1254.

- Love children completely from infancy to prevent impulsive behaviors in adolescence, i.e. behaviors that occur instantly without considering the outcome.
- Practice teaching children to wait, especially after the age of four. For example, when a child is hungry, teach the child to wait until the meal is ready. Moreover, a child can wait until his parent can afford to buy a toy and it is appropriate to wait one's turn when playing games with other children.
- Children are taught self-control when parents enforce rules at home. A child may not appreciate the rules and this lack of appreciation can be handled by the parent kindly saying, "I love you and it is too early for you to have a cell phone. We will talk about a cell phone when you are older."
- A parent should be a good role model for the child in difficult or anger-inducing situations. A parent can model remaining calm when anger is the easier emotion to exhibit. The child will learn this calm behavior when it is patterned by the parent.
- Parents may reward a child's good behavior – especially when the child had forgone an immediate or unhealthy pleasure. Keep in mind that rewards do not require the purchase of a toy or other monetary expense. The parent can offer to extend an activity that is restricted such as watching TV longer than usually permitted.

Parents can teach their children to ignore an immediate or unhealthy pleasure in order to achieve a better condition in the future.

Strengthening Executive Functions

The executive functions are known as the brain conductor and they function much like the air traffic controller at a busy airport.

The executive functions are brain advanced and high-level skills developed from infancy.[1] The control center is in the brain behind the forehead. Executive functions enable children to solve problems, plan, focus, concentrate, successfully perform multiple tasks, control emotions and exhibit self-control and flexible thinking. Research indicates adults whose executive functions are not adequately developed during childhood are more likely to abuse drugs and alcohol as adults.[2]

---

[1] Blair C. Executive function and early childhood education. Current Opinion in Behavioral Sciences. 2016 Aug 1;10:102-7.
[2] Wilens TE, Martelon M, Fried R, Petty C, Bateman C, Biederman J. Do executive function deficits predict later substance use disorders among adolescents and young adults?. Journal of the American Academy of Child & Adolescent Psychiatry. 2011 Feb 1;50(2):141-9.

Executive functions also have a direct relationship to children's academic achievement and learning.[1]

Children with executive dysfunction:
- Are impulsive instead of thinking first and then acting (Impulse Control)
- Have less control over their emotions; for example, they become sad or angry after an insignificant criticism. (Emotional Control)
- Do not show flexibility in their thinking and cannot consider something from different aspects; they can be very stubborn; like a mule. (Flexible Thinking)
- Have poor learning memory (Working Memory)
- Have less control of their behaviors and do not consider the consequences of their actions. For example, if they receive bad grades, they cannot measure what part their behavior played in the receipt of those grades. (Self-Monitoring)
- Are not able to prioritize their plans and cannot understand which parts of the plans are most important. (Planning and Prioritizing)
- Get confused and disappointed when beginning a task. (Task Initiation)

---

[1] Blair C. Executive function and early childhood education. Current Opinion in Behavioral Sciences. 2016 Aug 1;10:102-7.

The executive functions, shaped from childhood, are like the air traffic controller at a busy airport.

A parent should consider the following strategies for the child under the age of eight [1] to reinforce executive functions as important drug and alcohol abuse prevention tools:

---

[1] Bowne J. Enhancing and practicing executive function skills with children from infancy to adolescence. Center on the Developing Child, Harvard University 2013.

- Between 6 and 18 months of age – the parent can help the child with tasks and gradually withdraw support as the child becomes more proficient. A parent can enhance the child's executive function by playing games such as peekaboo and hide-and-find and by encouraging the child to imitate the parent's tasks. Loving children are the result of appropriate wiring of the brain paths, especially in the prefrontal cortex, which is the origin of executive functions.
- Between 18 and 36 months of age – this is the age when speech rapidly develops. Storytelling, teaching object names and playing singing games with many movements are effective for enhancing executive functions.
- Between 3 and 5 years of age – this is the time of rapid development of executive functions. Within this age range, it is important for the children to feel they can complete tasks without help. Playing and storytelling are two essential tools to enhance executive functions. Puzzles are helpful if they are age appropriate. Hiking is also beneficial for executive functions development.
- Between 5 and 7 years of age – Children enjoy games with rules and games requiring accuracy and quick response. Moreover, logic, reasoning and guessing games can be played at this age.

Reinforce the Assertiveness and skill of Saying "NO"

Many teenagers, when offered drugs or alcohol, cannot say "NO" because shyness causes them to be afraid of annoying their friends or facing ridicule.[1] Such adolescents are likely to abuse drugs and alcohol. Therefore, parents must reinforce children's assertiveness from early childhood -before the child reaches school age- through storytelling and role-playing.[2] The prerequisite for this skill building exercise is a warm and intimate parent-child relationship. Children must have a negative viewpoint of drugs and alcohol based on the behavior modeled by the parents.[3]

Parents teach their children, through storytelling and role-play, that saying "NO" to those who offer risky behavior is a sign of courage not cowardliness or weakness.

---

[1] Rahim M, Patton R. The association between shame and substance use in young people: a systematic review. PeerJ. 2015 Jan 22;3:e737.
[2] Dickinson DM, Hayes KA, Jackson C, Ennett ST, Lawson C. Promoting an alcohol-free childhood: A novel home-based parenting program. American journal of health education. 2014 Mar 1;45(2):119-28.
[3] Andreas JB, Pape H, Bretteville-Jensen AL. Who are the adolescents saying "No" to cannabis offers. Drug and alcohol dependence. 2016 Jun 1;163:64-70.

Peer Influence

It has been clearly shown the likelihood of drug and alcohol abuse increases in adolescents whose friends consume drugs and alcohol.[1,2]

Therefore, it is advisable to know the children's friends.[3] Not only should parents know their children's close friends, but also know the friend's parents.[4] It is always important to share negative viewpoints regarding drugs and alcohol with parents of your child's friends.

Parents should know their children's friends and the friend's parents. Moreover, parents should develop friendships with families whose behaviors are not harmful to the children.

---

[1] Nakhaee N, Jadidi N. Why do some teens turn to drugs? a focus group study of drug users' experiences. Journal of Addictions Nursing. 2009 Nov 12;20(4):203-8.

[2] Mrug S, McCay R. Parental and peer disapproval of alcohol use and its relationship to adolescent drinking: Age, gender, and racial differences. Psychology of Addictive Behaviors. 2013 Sep;27(3):604.

[3] Rusby JC, Light JM, Crowley R, Westling E. Influence of parent–youth relationship, parental monitoring, and parent substance use on adolescent substance use onset. Journal of family psychology. 2018 Apr;32(3):310.

[4] Cleveland MJ, Feinberg ME, Osgood DW, Moody J. Do peers' parents matter? A new link between positive parenting and adolescent substance use. Journal of studies on alcohol and drugs. 2012 May;73(3):423-33.

Do not overlook the impact of films

Cultural norms and beliefs are one of the important factors for adolescent's drug and alcohol abuse.[1] Films are one of the influences that form children's attitudes toward various substances, from tobacco to marijuana and alcohol. Alcohol and tobacco industries use digital media as an effective way to interest children in consuming their products.[2] Not only do children consider drinking alcohol a normal activity by watching films that promote alcohol directly and indirectly, but they become curious about alcohol. Therefore, it is best for parents to preview movies before allowing children to watch. Even with children who do not have predisposing factors to alcoholism, watching scenes of alcohol use on television and digital devices make them susceptible to alcohol at an early age.[3]

---

[1] Sudhinaraset M, Wigglesworth C, Takeuchi DT. Social and cultural contexts of alcohol use: Influences in a social–ecological framework. Alcohol research: current reviews. 2016.

[2] Strasburger VC. Policy statement--children, adolescents, substance abuse, and the media. Pediatrics. 2010 Oct;126(4):791-9.

[3] Hanewinkel R, Sargent JD, Hunt K, Sweeting H, Engels RC, Scholte RH, Mathis F, Florek E, Morgenstern M. Portrayal of alcohol consumption in movies and drinking initiation in low-risk adolescents. Pediatrics. 2014 Jun 1;133(6):973-82.

Parents need to be careful to avoid scenes with drug and alcohol abuse transmitted through movies and digital media.

Nurture the Child's Spirituality

Religious beliefs have a protective role in drug and alcohol use.[1] This protective effect is significant in adulthood especially if children are raised with these beliefs from early childhood.[2] According to Miller:

---

[1] Park CL, Masters KS, Salsman JM, Wachholtz A, Clements AD, Salmoirago-Blotcher E, Trevino K, Wischenka DM. Advancing our understanding of religion and spirituality in the context of behavioral medicine. Journal of behavioral medicine. 2017 Feb 1;40(1):39-51.

[2] Porche M, Fortuna L, Wachholtz A, Stone R. Distal and proximal religiosity as protective factors for adolescent and emerging adult alcohol use. Religions. 2015 Jun;6(2):365-84.

"Spirituality is the central organizing principle of inner life" later in adolescence.[1] A personal sense of spirituality protects children from drug and alcohol abuse.

Parents should incorporate spirituality into their children's lives and promote morals such as truthfulness, sympathy and gratitude. Parents speaking about their own moral behavior will improve children's spirituality.

Parents should talk to their children about God and his kindness, especially in nature. If prayer is part of the parent's life, the parent should do spiritual practice before the child.

To promote spirituality in children, love them and be a positive role model in terms of adhering to morality and praising God in everyday life.

---

[1] Miller L. The spiritual child: The new science on parenting for health and lifelong thriving. Macmillan; 2016 May 10.